Handwriting
Activity Book

for ages 9-10

This CGP book is bursting with fun activities to build up children's skills and confidence.

It's ideal for extra practice to reinforce what they're learning in primary school. Enjoy!

 # Handwriting Hints

Here are some tips to help you keep your writing neat:

1. Make sure your writing rests on the line.

2. Try to keep the spaces between words even.

3. Don't rush. Take your time and concentrate on keeping your writing as neat and tidy as possible.

4. Letters of the same type should be the same size:
   - small letters (like c and o) should all be the same height
   - the tops of tall letters (like k and l) should go up to the same height
   - the tails on letters like g and y should be the same length

5. Remember that a 't' is a bit shorter than tall letters.

6. Capital letters should be the same height as tall letters.

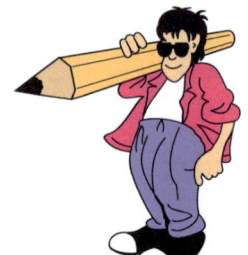

7. Keep the downstrokes of letters straight and make sure they tilt by the same amount.

Every school has its own handwriting style. Some schools may form letters and joins differently to how they're written here. Check with the school to see how they write and join each letter.

Contents

Alphabet practice	2
More alphabet practice	4
Modal verbs	6
Silent letters	8
Word endings	10
More word endings	12
Puzzle: Library dilemma	14
Noun phrases	16
Relative clauses	18
Vegetable report	20
Winter poems	22
A musical letter	24
Luke's tale of riches	26
Hippo fact file	28
Answers	30

Published by CGP

Editors: Andy Cashmore,
Helen Clements, Rachel Craig-McFeely,
Becca Lakin, Nathan Mair

With thanks to Alex Fairer and
Alison Griffin for the proofreading.

With thanks to Alice Dent
for the copyright research.

ISBN: 978 1 83774 039 0

Printed by Elanders Ltd, Newcastle upon Tyne.
Graphics used on the cover and throughout the book from Corel®
Cover design concept by emc design ltd.

Text, design, layout and original illustrations
© Coordination Group Publications Ltd. (CGP) 2023
All rights reserved.

Photocopying this book is not permitted, even if you have a CLA licence.
Extra copies are available from CGP with next day delivery • 0800 1712 712 • www.cgpbooks.co.uk

Alphabet practice

How It Works

Here's some alphabet practice to kick things off. The words on these pages all start with letters from the first half of the alphabet.

Make sure that your writing rests on the lines and remember to watch out for break letters and capital letters.

Now Try These

1. Can you copy out the phrases below?

   aloof ants   blissful beach

      crying child   deep dive   elf ear

   fun films   guilty goldfish   huge hotel

2. Now have a go at copying out these longer phrases.

   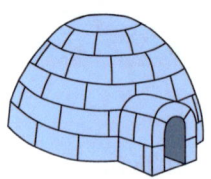   icy indoor igloo

   jazzy jam jar

   kind knitting king

   lazy lions lie

   many magic mackerel

3. Can you copy out the sentences for some more practice of the first half of the alphabet?

My cousin always loses her car keys.

I am exploring a fascinating jungle.

A clumsy fairy flopped into my bedroom.

He has dark green eyes and brown hair.

Kangaroos like jumping and eating grass.

An Extra Challenge

Niall needs to write a short passage for his homework. He's thought of some words to include, but now he's struggling to put them into sentences. Can you help him by writing some sentences which include the words below?

horse
bizarre
intrepid
cryptic
leotard
elephant
kite
danced
gravy
minuscule
artist
jumped
flew

Did you ace the alphabet?
Tick one of the boxes.

More alphabet practice

How It Works

Nice work! It's time to practise copying letters from the second half of the alphabet.

Remember to write on the lines and watch out for break letters.

Now Try These

1. Copy out each of the phrases twice on the lines.

    nosy newt

    ornate oven

    proud princess

    quirky quiz

    rapid robin

    slime soup

2. Can you copy out these longer phrases that start with the last letters of the alphabet?

    ten tall trees   *ugly useless umbrella*

    very vigilant villain   *wild white wolf*

    your yellow yacht   *zero zebra zone*

3. Practise the second half of the alphabet by copying out the sentences.

The vet will need to x-ray the owl's wing.

She vowed to play the xylophone regularly.

 *Queen Sara rode your new pony.*

Rockets zoomed through space.

The view out of the window was unbelievable.

An Extra Challenge

There are thirteen pupils in your class. Each name starts with a different letter from the second half of the alphabet.

Write a list of their names, and an adjective to describe each of them.

You should only use adjectives that start with letters from the second half of the alphabet. Try to use as many different letters as you can.

You can use the adjectives on the whiteboard to help you.

Are you amazing at the alphabet? Give a box a tick.

Modal verbs

How It Works

Modal verbs show how likely something is to happen. They can also be used to ask questions.

might   **should**   **will**

less certain ⟶ more certain

Now Try These

1. Can you copy out each of these modal verbs twice on the lines below?

   shall   *might*

   may   *could*

   can   *would*

2. Can you copy out the conversation below on the lines?

   Must we drink this terrible tea?

   I think we should.

   I shall vomit!

   I might just eat sugar.

3. Copy out each of the sentences to show what Toby is thinking of doing today.

It will be a gloriously sunny day today.

I could go outside and play in the garden...

...although then I would need a bath.

I really must avoid that at all costs!

A nap on the sofa may be better for me.

An Extra Challenge

Look at the scene below. Can you use the prompts in the boxes to write four sentences that describe what might happen next? Make sure you use joined up writing.

The cat must...

That ball might...

They should...

I think it will...

I would love it if you could please put a tick in a box.

Silent letters

How It Works

Silent letters are letters in words that you don't say out loud.

write   **design**   **climb**

You don't pronounce the green letters in these words.

Now Try These

1. These words all contain silent letters. Copy them out on the lines below.

   scissors 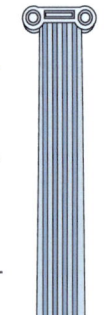 rustle 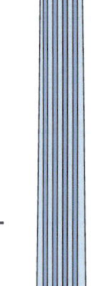 knock 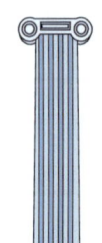 guilt

   column   school   assign   psychic

2. Can you copy out the phrases on the lines below?

   swords in a castle

   the science of knots

   guitar in a cupboard

   a wreath of thistles

   the butcher's receipt

    island of gnomes

   wretched disguise

3. Copy out the sentences below. Can you circle all the words with silent letters?

You should slice the raspberries with a knife.

It's doubtful that this scene will fascinate you.

He hurt his thumb and wrist on Wednesday.

The whole business is chaotic at Christmas.

Why are there crumbs in the biscuit aisle?

An Extra Challenge

Penelope has found part of a story in a book but some of the silent letters have smudged.

Can you copy out the passage in joined up writing, adding the silent letters in the gaps?

Her mus⎸les ac⎸ed as she ran through the ⎸narled trees of the forest. Suddenly, she cou⎸d see a w⎸ite b⎸ilding ahead. She ran inside and ⎸nelt on the floor. This wou⎸d make a perfect hiding spot.

How did you find the silent letters? Put a tick in a box.

Word endings

How It Works

Some word endings sound similar but are spelt differently, such as -ible and -able.

visible   mixable

The endings -tious and -cious also sound similar but are spelt differently.

Now Try These

1. Copy out these phrases.

   ferocious lion

   ambitious antelope

   adorably cute

   sensibly done

   capable cowboy

2. Here are some longer phrases to copy out.

   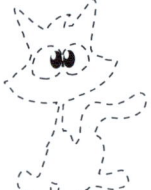

   an invisible cat   *your infectious bug*

   the vicious dog   *an atrocious storm*

   his inedible food   *her valuable pearl*

3. Have a go at copying out these sentences.

The grass in the spacious field is nutritious.

 *Pilots are always terribly cautious.*

Lei the gymnast is undeniably flexible.

4. Here is a longer sentence. Write it out as neatly as possible.

Tony is a notably excitable chimpanzee, but the horrible noise he makes is unbearable.

An Extra Challenge

Here is a diary entry, but some of the letters in the bold words have been mixed up. Can you unscramble the words in bold and write them out in joined up writing?

The party food was **ylcrediinb** tasty. The cheese sandwiches were **iledcusio**. The cake was very **sibaezle** and tasted **muscrutipos**. I don't think it would have been **sopslibe** for me to have eaten more! It was **lybrapob** the best party I've been to.

Now rewrite the diary entry in your neatest handwriting.

Are you incredible at writing word endings? Tick a box.

More word endings

How It Works

Several more common word endings sound similar but are spelt differently, for example:

audience   entrance

Now Try These

1. Copy out these phrases which use some common word endings.

   really long distance

   green cement mixer

   their special surprise

   very high buoyancy

   rickety wooden fence

2. Can you copy out these short sentences?

   His pace is glacial.   The rain is torrential.

   She is his parent.   Do you like science?

   I lost my balance and fell over.

3. Now write out these sentences. How many common word endings can you spot?

What a brilliant sentence this is!

She overcame her initial hesitancy.

I believe that blackcurrant squash is essential.

4. Have a go at copying out this longer sentence.

The vigilant officers in the spy agency go to every emergency.

An Extra Challenge

Diana the dentist has made a poster with some teeth tips, but she's forgotten to use spaces. Can you write out the tips in joined writing, putting spaces in the right places?

How many common word endings can you find on the poster?

TOP TEETH TIPS

Patientsshouldgoto thedentistonceayear.

Mintytoothpaste makesyourmouth morefragrant.

Accordingtoevidenceyou shouldbrushfortwominutes.

Itiscrucialthatyoubrush yourteethtwiceaday.

Avoidingsugarisimportant fortoothmaintenance.

Are you content with these word endings? Tick a box.

Library dilemma

The library books on the table have been mixed up! Work out which book each child has borrowed by completing the tasks in the speech bubbles. Use the book covers and the titles to help you. Make sure you use your neatest joined up writing for your answers.

Fill in the missing silent letters in the sentence below. Then write the full sentence on the lines.

The main c[ ]aracter is a wi[ ]ch who g[ ]ards a s[ ]ord in a tom[ ].

_____
_____
_____

The sentence below is written backwards. Rewrite the sentence the right way round.

The title of my book starts with the last letter of the alphabet.

_____
_____
_____

Rewrite this sentence with the right spacing.

Mycoverisfloral.

_____
_____

Cam

Tina

Max

The words in each box can be rearranged to make a relative clause. Unscramble each relative clause, then write the sentence on the lines.

My tale, [under sea which set is the], is about a queen [Isla whose is name].

_____
_____

Kofi

Unscramble the bold words, then rewrite the sentence on the lines.

It's a moving **tlea** of a **guyon** boy and a **miitd** wolf cub **ggnwori** up together in a **trefos**.

_____
_____
_____
_____

Cross out the wrong spelling of the words in the boxes, then rewrite the whole sentence, using the right spellings.

The plot was terrable / terrible : it was about an elephant / elephent who was a nuisance / nuisence .

_____
_____
_____
_____

You're on the write track!

Diya

LIBRARY

Zinnia the Knight • The Hidden Blade • Troublesome Trunk • Life Amidst Trees • Soft Yellow Petals • Ruler of Mermaids

Eva

Write the titles of the books next to the names of the children that have borrowed them.

Tina — _____

Max — _____

Cam — _____

Kofi — _____

Diya — _____

Eva — _____

Noun phrases

How It Works

Noun phrases contain a noun and any words that describe that noun.
You can make noun phrases longer by adding adjectives, prepositions or more nouns.

that defiant **dog** *with a bone*

↑ words added to noun ↑ noun ↑ words added to noun

Now Try These

1. Can you copy out these short noun phrases?

   my rickety bicycle

   his talkative parrot

   the stormy clouds

   our palatial house

2. Now have a go at copying out these longer noun phrases.

   a blue lorry behind us   *my jacket on the peg*

   their beautiful, expensive painting on the wall

   her creaking bookcase full of large novels

3. Copy out these sentences that contain noun phrases.
   Can you underline each of the noun phrases?

   My relaxing holiday at the beach has ended.

   The chunky hamster with the banana is happy.

   I make delicious chocolate cakes at home.

4. See if you can copy out this short passage onto the lines below.

   The golden trophy in my hands was gorgeous.
   My bitter rival for first place chased after me.

An Extra Challenge

Nadine is looking to hire a speedy writer for her magazine.
She will only hire someone who can beat her time at writing the passage below.
Copy the passage as quickly and neatly as you can, using joined up writing.

Nadine's Time:

4:00

The athletic runner with a tight vest sprinted quickly. He was close behind the tall woman who was focused on the thin, red tape in the distance. Suddenly, the large crowd cheered loudly, as the man in second place overtook the exhausted woman.

Can you underline all of the noun phrases that appear in this passage?

Were you fazed by noun phrases? Tick a box.

Relative clauses

How It Works

A relative clause is a type of subordinate clause — it adds extra information to a sentence.

Relative clauses are often introduced by relative pronouns, e.g. 'who', 'whose', 'that' or 'which'.

I use a machine **which** is old.

↑ relative pronoun
↑ relative clause

You can also use the words 'when' and 'where' to introduce relative clauses.

Now Try These

1. Underline the relative clause in each sentence. Then copy the sentences.

   Hal, whose violin was stolen, is very angry.

   Kit will buy more soap when we run out.

   Nicki, who enjoys basketball, is at a game.

   Akira likes the shop that is run by the iguana.

   Let's go to the beach where we first met.

2. Have a go at copying this short passage onto the lines below.

May is making a stew which will taste bad.
She plans to add radishes that are mouldy.

3. Now copy this longer passage out.

Rob has golf clubs which are really old.
He was given them by Lola, who is his sister.
One of the clubs snapped when he last played.

An Extra Challenge

Ralph is doing a brain teaser. Can you help him connect the right sentence starter to each relative clause? Write out the complete sentences, using your neatest joined up writing.

Vivian is a young explorer	when she visited the Amazon rainforest.
She discovered a hidden temple	where she has a house in Athens.
Her favourite meal is a burger	who loves seeing new places.
She likes to relax in Greece	which has extra mayonnaise.

Did these pages go relatively well for you? Tick a box.

Vegetable report

How It Works

You've made some amazing progress with joined up writing. Now it's time to practise writing out some longer passages.

Use your handwriting skills to copy this newspaper article. Can you spot the modal verbs and relative clauses?

Now Try These

1. Copy out the first few sentences of the newspaper article.

   Disaster struck in Kaletown on Sunday when an award-winning leek was reported missing.

   Farmer Bryan's leek, which was over a metre long, had won the village's vegetable contest.

   Many attendees claimed that Farmer Efe, who won the previous year, may be to blame.

2. Now try copying out the rest of the article onto the lines below.

Others suggested that it must have been eaten, after rumours circulated of a goat at the scene. Mr Plum, whose turnip came last, said they should crown a different victor. However, it is unlikely the judges will allow this. A full investigation is due to take place.

An Extra Challenge

Can you write a newspaper article based on the events depicted in the scenes below?
Try to include some modal verbs and relative clauses in your writing.
Remember to give your article a headline and use your neatest handwriting.

Were these pages newsworthy?
Tick a box to show how you did.

Winter poems

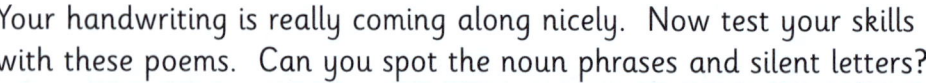

How It Works

Your handwriting is really coming along nicely. Now test your skills with these poems. Can you spot the noun phrases and silent letters?

Now Try These

1. Copy the first three lines of the poem on the lines below.

   I walk outside to a blanket of snow,
   Which glistens under the moon's bright glow,
   Covering all of the plants below.

2. Have a go at copying the rest of the poem.

   A magical sight brimming with glee:
   Icicles hang from the holly tree.
   I pirouette, my joy running free,
   My footprints the first in this wintry sea.

3. Circle the words with silent letters. Then copy out the poem.

> Retreating from the cold outdoors,
> To a cosy room where a fire roars.
> Twinkling lights hang from each wall,
> And laughter echoes down the hall.
> Thick woolly socks embrace my toes,
> Outside a stormy gale blows.
> How we'll get home? Nobody knows.

An Extra Challenge

Copy out the first two lines of the poem in the blue box and finish it by writing the third and fourth lines. The third line should rhyme with the first line, and the fourth line should rhyme with the second. Use noun phrases and some of the silent letter words in the box.

> Skiing and ice skating with my friends,
> Winter brings endless amounts of fun.

wreath   listen
numb

Can you write a second verse? Try to use the same rhyme scheme.

Did you do brrr-illiantly?
Tick one of the boxes.

A musical letter

How It Works

Impressive work so far. It's time for some more practice.

Put everything you've learnt to the test with this letter. It includes lots of modal verbs.

Now Try These

1. Start by copying out the first part of the letter onto the lines below.

Imran Qadir
7 Bluebell Lane
Rivergate

Dear Adam,
You won't believe what happened last night!
On my way to trumpet practice, I saw my
favourite singer, Mila Sky, in the town square.

Answers

Here are the answers to the Extra Challenges and puzzle. All answers should be written in joined up writing.

Pages 2-3 — Alphabet practice

Any sensible sentences using the words given, e.g. The <u>intrepid</u> <u>elephant</u> <u>danced</u> with a <u>horse</u>.

Pages 4-5 — More alphabet practice

You should have written a list of 13 names and adjectives starting with the second thirteen letters of the alphabet, e.g. zany Zach

Pages 6-7 — Modal verbs

Any sensible sentences that describe the scene using the prompts given, e.g. The cat must climb the tree to escape the dog.

Pages 8-9 — Silent letters

Her mus<u>c</u>les a<u>c</u>hed as she ran through the <u>g</u>narled trees of the forest. Suddenly, she cou<u>l</u>d see a <u>w</u>hite <u>b</u>uilding ahead. She ran inside and <u>k</u>nelt on the floor. This wou<u>l</u>d make a perfect hiding spot.

Pages 10-11 — Word endings

The party food was <u>incredibly</u> tasty. The cheese sandwiches were <u>delicious</u>. The cake was very <u>sizeable</u> and tasted <u>scrumptious</u>. I don't think it would have been <u>possible</u> for me to have eaten more! It was <u>probably</u> the best party I've been to.

Pages 12-13 — More word endings

Patients should go to the dentist once a year.
Minty toothpaste makes your mouth more fragrant.
According to evidence you should brush for two minutes.
It is crucial that you brush your teeth twice a day.
Avoiding sugar is important for tooth maintenance.

Pages 14-15 — Library dilemma

Tina: The main <u>c</u>haracter is a wit<u>c</u>h who <u>g</u>uards a s<u>w</u>ord in a tom<u>b</u>.
Max: The title of my book starts with the last letter of the alphabet.
Cam: My cover is floral.
Kofi: My tale, <u>which is set under the sea</u>, is about a queen <u>whose name is Isla</u>.
Diya: It's a moving <u>tale</u> of a <u>young</u> boy and a <u>timid</u> wolf cub <u>growing</u> up together in a <u>forest</u>.
Eva: The plot was <u>terrible</u>: it was about an <u>elephant</u> who was a <u>nuisance</u>.

Tina — The Hidden Blade
Max — Zinnia the Knight
Cam — Soft Yellow Petals
Kofi — Ruler of Mermaids
Diya — Life Amidst Trees
Eva — Troublesome Trunk

Pages 16-17 — Noun phrases

You should have underlined: The athletic runner with a tight vest; the tall woman; the thin, red tape in the distance; the large crowd; the man in second place; the exhausted woman

Pages 18-19 — Relative clauses

Vivian is a young explorer who loves seeing new places. She discovered a hidden temple when she visited the Amazon rainforest. Her favourite meal is a burger which has extra mayonnaise. She likes to relax in Greece where she has a house in Athens.

Pages 20-21 — Vegetable report

You should have written a newspaper report which describes how a farmer lost his favourite pig, then found her in a swimming pool. It should have a headline and use modal verbs and relative clauses.
E.g. <u>Missing Pig Found In Swimming Pool</u>
Roncaster Leisure Centre has been told it must improve its security after a pig that had escaped from a nearby farm was found relaxing in the swimming pool.

Pages 22-23 — Winter poems

Any sensible two lines to finish the poem. The third line should rhyme with the first and the fourth with the second. It should use noun phrases and some of the silent letter words given.
E.g. <u>Listen</u> to carols and skid around bends,
     Then warm our <u>numb</u> fingers in the winter sun.

You should have also written a second verse that continues the poem and follows the same rhyme scheme.

Pages 24-25 — A musical letter

You should have written a letter about Adam meeting his favourite celebrity, using the address and modal verbs given.
E.g.
                Adam Smith
                16 High Street
                Crinton

Dear Imran,
I <u>should</u> tell you about when I met my favourite actor.

Pages 26-27 — Luke's tale of riches

You should have written a paragraph that continues the story based on one of the prompts given.
E.g. A large, angry-looking giant in a suit of armour entered the room. Luke hid behind a pile of coins as the giant cast his eyes around the mountains of shiny treasure.

Pages 28-29 — Hippo fact file

You should have written a fact file about an imaginary animal. E.g. Squirumps can be found in forests across Europe and Asia. They have a varied diet of mushrooms, leaves and small insects.

(lined writing space)

An Extra Challenge

Can you write your own fact file about an imaginary animal?

Mention where they live, what they eat and any other interesting facts.

Remember to use neat joined up writing.

Report back on how these pages went by putting a tick in a box.

Hippo fact file

How It Works

Fantastic work! This non-fiction report is your last bit of handwriting practice.

Look out for numbers in the report — they should be as tall as capital letters.

Now Try This

1. Read this fact file about hippos. Can you copy it out onto the next page?

   Hippos, one of the largest land mammals, live in sub-Saharan Africa. Although they spend up to 16 hours a day in water, their swimming technique is unusual (they mostly walk and glide along the river bed). Incredibly, they can hold their breath for up to 5 minutes.

   Despite their cuddly looks, hippos are highly dangerous animals. They can weigh over 2 tonnes, are surprisingly fast and have extremely sharp teeth. Fortunately, they are herbivores and mostly eat grass.

   Sadly, hippo populations are declining. Threats to their survival — such as loss of habitat and poaching — led to them being classified as a vulnerable species in 2016.

2. Now have a go at copying out the second part of the story.

Luke spotted a sizeable ruby nestled at the base of a towering pile of coins. It was as large as a fist and shone like a juicy red apple, ripe for picking. Luke knew it was special. Yet as he dislodged the gem, the coins above started to slide with such force that the floor rumbled. Hearing urgent footsteps, Luke audibly gulped.

An Extra Challenge

What do you think happens next? In your neatest joined up writing, write a paragraph to continue the story using one of these prompts.

Try to use some longer noun phrases in your descriptions.

Luke manages to hide and slip away with the ruby.

The angry giant finds Luke and chases him.

Quick! Tick a box before the giant catches up with you.

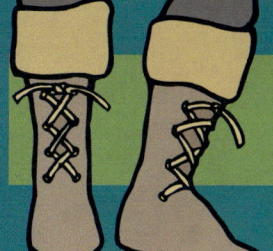

Luke's tale of riches

How It Works

Great job! Now practise your handwriting with a short story.

Look out for noun phrases and word endings.

Now Try These

1. Copy out these passages from the story on the lines below.

    Luke stared in awe at the brilliant sight. The cavernous hall was full of coins and precious gemstones. The giant must have been stealing riches from hundreds of villages for centuries.

    Luke shook with uncontrollable rage. How could the cruel, selfish giant be so greedy? Luke needed evidence to show his village.

2. Read the rest of the letter and circle the modal verbs. Then copy it out.

I couldn't believe it! She must have been filming her new music video — there were cameras everywhere and people dressed as witches. I should have asked Mila for her autograph, but I thought I might get in the way. I shall tell you all about it next month. From Imran

An Extra Challenge

Imagine you are Adam. Write a reply to Imran's letter to tell him about the time you met your favourite celebrity. Include Adam's address and the modal verbs below.

should   may   would   shall   must

Adam Smith
16 High Street
Crinton

Think carefully about the tone of your letter and remember to use your neatest joined up writing.

Were you pitch-perfect on those pages? Tick one of the boxes.